T0056994

Cecilia McDowall

O Antiphon Sequence

for solo organ

MUSIC DEPARTMENT

OXFORD
UNIVERSITY PRESS

Composer's note

Each of the seven movements of *O Antiphon Sequence* is structured on one of the seven notes of the diatonic scale in a 'circle of fifths' formation, and each individual movement is a response to a short extract of liturgical text taken from the O Antiphons.

In the first of the seven, *O Sapientia*, I have taken the phrase '… mightily and sweetly ordering all things'; this antiphon moves steadily onwards, alternating between *dolce* melodies and more robust passages.

I have based *O Adonai* on '… in the flame of the burning bush'. In contrast to the previous movement, this is lively, flickering, and capricious.

Thoughtful and meditative, *O Radix Jesse* draws on the text '… to you the nations will make their prayer'. The continuum of the offbeat pedal D is set against falling and rising expressive chromatic phrases.

The words '… you open and none may close' usher in a bright, open, and uplifting toccata, *O Clavis David*.

O Oriens is allied to my a cappella setting of this antiphon. In the luminous key of E major, the block, sometimes dissonant, chords progress to a *forte* climax, then the texture pulls back to a more thoughtful conclusion: '… come and enlighten those that dwell in darkness'.

Rooted and firm, *O Rex Gentium* ('… the cornerstone making both one') moves at a steady pace, overlaid with a highly decorated melodic line.

In each of the antiphons so far there have been intimations of the O Antiphon plainchant, either in the pedal or within the texture of the work. In this, the final O Antiphon, *O Emmanuel*, I have used another plainchant, *O come, O come, Emmanuel*, and bound this beautiful ancient melody to the text '… come to save us, O Lord our God'. The opening little motive, based on notes from the opening phrase of the hymn, makes a repeated appearance throughout this movement in, I hope, an evocative way. Below the bell-like motif the re-harmonised chords of the hymn advance, haltingly at times. The short motif concludes the sequence, suspended in mid-air.

Designed to be performed as a recital piece, *O Antiphon Sequence* should work just as well performed as individual movements within a liturgical context. *O Antiphon Sequence* has been commissioned and generously funded by the American Guild of Organists. It was first performed by Vincent Dubois on 3 July 2018 at the AGO National Convention in Kansas City, Missouri.

Duration: 14'30"   © Cecilia McDowall, 2018

Commissioned by the American Guild of Organists

O Antiphon Sequence

1. O Sapientia

Sw.: Trompette (or Oboe)
Gt.: Flute 8'
Ped.: Diapason 16', 8'

CECILIA McDOWALL

'…fortiter suaviterque disponens omnia'
'…mightily and sweetly ordering all things'

© Oxford University Press 2018

Printed in Great Britain

OXFORD UNIVERSITY PRESS, MUSIC DEPARTMENT, GREAT CLARENDON STREET, OXFORD OX2 6DP
The Moral Rights of the Composer have been asserted. Photocopying this copyright material is ILLEGAL.

2. O Adonai

CECILIA McDOWALL

Sw.: Full
Gt.: to Mixture, Sw. to Gt.
Ped.: Full

'...in igne flammae rubi'
'...in the flame of the burning bush'

3. O Radix Jesse

Sw.: Soft Foundations, Celeste
Gt.: 8', 4' (clear)
Ped.: Soft 16', 8' uncoupled

'...quem Gentes deprecabuntur'
'...to you the nations will make their prayer'

CECILIA McDOWALL

4. O Clavis David

Sw.: Full
Gt.: to Mixture, Sw. to Gt.
Ped.: Full

'...qui aperis, et nemo claudit'
'...you open and none may close'

CECILIA McDOWALL

5. O Oriens

Sw.: Flutes 8', 4', 2'
Gt.: to Mixture
Ped.: 16', 8', 4', Sw. to Ped.

'...veni, et illumina sedentes in tenebris'
'...come and enlighten those who dwell in darkness'

CECILIA McDOWALL

Radiant, luminous ♩ = 40

6. O Rex Gentium

Sw.: Flutes 8', 4', Trompette
Gt.: Flute 8'
Ped.: Diapason 16', 8'

'...lapisque angularis, qui facis utraque unum'   CECILIA McDOWALL
'...the cornerstone making both one'

7. O Emmanuel

Sw.: Diapason and Flute 8' (warm)
Gt.: Flutes 8' & 4' (clear)
Ped.: Diapason 16', Flutes 16', 8' uncoupled

'...veni ad salvandum nos, Domine, Deus noster.'
'...come to save us, O Lord our God.'

CECILIA McDOWALL